KU-414-798

Play Strindberg

by the same author

plays

THE VISIT

FOUR PLAYS
The Marriage of Mr Mississippi
An Angel Comes to Babylon
The Physicists
Romulus the Great

fiction

THE PLEDGE

A DANGEROUS GAME

ONCE A GREEK ...

THE JUDGE AND HIS HANGMAN

Play Strindberg

THE DANCE OF DEATH

CHOREOGRAPHED

BY FRIEDRICH DÜRRENMATT

Translated from the German by
JAMES KIRKUP

James Kirkup

JONATHAN CAPE
THIRTY BEDFORD SQUARE LONDON

TRANSLATED FROM THE GERMAN *Play Strindberg*
© 1969 BY PETER SCHIFFERLI, VERLAGS AG 'DIE ARCHE', ZURICH
THIS TRANSLATION FIRST PUBLISHED IN GREAT BRITAIN 1972
TRANSLATION © 1972 BY JONATHAN CAPE LTD

JONATHAN CAPE LTD, 30 BEDFORD SQUARE, LONDON WCI

ISBN 0 224 00727 0

This play is fully protected by copyright.
All inquiries concerning performing rights in Great Britain
and the Commonwealth, professional or amateur, should
be directed to Dr Jan van Loewen Ltd, International Copyright Agency, 81–83 Shaftesbury Avenue, London W1V 8BX

PRINTED IN GREAT BRITAIN BY
EBENEZER BAYLIS & SON LTD
THE TRINITY PRESS, WORCESTER, AND LONDON
ON PAPER MADE BY JOHN DICKINSON & CO. LTD
BOUND BY G. AND J. KITCAT LTD, LONDON

Characters

ALICE
EDGAR
KURT

Note

I saw Strindberg's *Dance of Death* in 1948, in Basle, with Maria Fein and Rudolf Forster; subsequently, memories of actors, but not of a play.

1968. Read the first pages of the play, found the dramatic idea interesting, but disliked its literariness (plush to the *n*th degree).

Tried a complete dramatic rewriting using short scenes, i.e. a dramatically viable reworking of Strindberg. Gave this up. Reason: the usual Strindberg reworkings with short scenes, transpositions, textual changes and textual expansions traduce Strindberg, which is all the more serious because in spite of all this it is claimed that Strindberg will be played in an 'authentic' style. An adaptation seems to me more honourable.

November 1968: began the adaptation using a rough translation.

From Strindberg I took the story and the dramatic idea. By eliminating the literary side of Strindberg, his dramatic vision becomes more sharply focused and more modern, related to Beckett, Ionesco or my own *Meteor*. Strindberg's dialogue was used as the starting-point of an anti-Strindberg dialogue — out of an actors' play I made a play for acting. The actor no longer needs to present studies of demonic obsessions, but has to make possible on the stage a text which has been depoeticized and deflated in the extreme.

December 1968: rehearsals began. The text was partly developed and altered during the work with the actors.

The final text emerged from an exhaustive examination of the various theatrical situations. The unison of a trio playing together with complete precision developed from the work of the three actors. The art of acting. Out of a bourgeois marriage tragedy developed a comedy about bourgeois marriage tragedies: *Play Strindberg*.

DÜRRENMATT

Translator's Note

In Herr Dürrenmatt's Note it is very difficult to convey the precise difference—if indeed there be any—between *Bearbeitung* and *Umarbeitung*, which I have translated respectively as 'reworking' or 'rewriting' and 'adaptation'. *Arrangiert* in Herr Dürrenmatt's subtitle suggests a musical rearrangement, and I have taken the liberty—since the word comes after *The Dance of Death*—to translate *arrangiert* ('arranged') as 'choreographed'. The title *Play Strindberg* is very odd, and seems to indicate an unfamiliarity on Dürrenmatt's part with English usage. I considered an alternative title, *Strindberg Without Tears*, which seemed very suitable for this 'bourgeois tragedy of marriage' that has been turned into a 'bourgeois comedy of marriage'.* And tears do make a brief appearance in Round Eleven, or so we are led to believe. But finally I rejected this as being too personal an interpretation.

Whether this version is a 'reworking', a 'rewriting', an 'adaptation' or an 'arrangement', it seems pretty clear to me that Dürrenmatt has relied heavily on Emil Schering's translation into German (not on a 'rough translation' as stated in the Note), first published in 1926. I can find little or no influence of Melchinger's 1948 translation, presumably the one Dürrenmatt saw in Basle in 1948.

I have made my own version of *Solveig's Song* to fit the music. On page 10 of the German text, *Kartenspiel!* is apparently a misprint for *Kartenspiel-szene 1*.

JAMES KIRKUP

Nagoya, Japan
June 1970

* Karl Marx in *The Eighteenth Brumaire of Louis Bonaparte* makes this comment on Hegel's remark that great historical events occur twice: 'Hegel forgot to add: the first time as tragedy, the second as farce.'

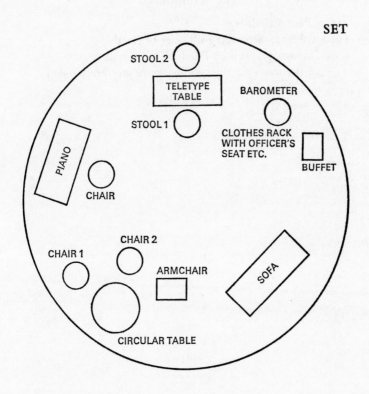

At the back and sides of this stage, black velvet curtains; on the boards a black velvet carpet. On this a light grey circular acting area. This contains various pieces of furniture. In the wings to left and right two property benches with the necessary props, which the actors fetch themselves. Above the acting area hangs a circular frame carrying spots. The stage manager strikes the gong.

Enter ALICE, EDGAR *and* KURT.

ALICE. Play Strindberg.
EDGAR. August Strindberg's 'Dance of Death'.
KURT. Choreographed by Friedrich Dürrenmatt.
(KURT *leaves the stage and sits on the prop bench right.*)

1

EDGAR. Round One.

ALICE. Conversation Before Dinner.

(*Gong.* ALICE *on the sofa, embroidering.* EDGAR *in the arm-chair. For a long time, nothing happens.* EDGAR *winds up his watch.*)

EDGAR. Play something.

ALICE. What?

EDGAR. Anything you like.

ALICE. *Solveig's Song.*

EDGAR. *The Entry of the Boyars.*

ALICE. You don't care for my repertoire.

EDGAR. Nor you for mine.

ALICE. Then I won't play anything.

(*Pause.*)

EDGAR. The door's open.

ALICE. Shall I shut it?

EDGAR. If you like.

ALICE. Then I won't shut it.

(*Pause.*)

ALICE. Smoke your cigar.

EDGAR. I can't stand these strong ones any more.

ALICE. Then smoke milder ones.

EDGAR. I haven't any milder ones.

ALICE. But smoking's the only happiness you get from life.

EDGAR. What is happiness?

ALICE. I don't know.

EDGAR. Me neither.

(*Pause.*)

ALICE. Whisky?

EDGAR. Later.

> (*Pause.*)

EDGAR. What's on tonight?

ALICE. Ask Jenny.

EDGAR. It's the start of the mackerel season.

ALICE. Is that so.

EDGAR. It's autumn.

ALICE. You're telling me.

EDGAR. A grilled mackerel with a slice of lemon wouldn't come amiss.

ALICE. All you think of now's your belly.

> (*Longer pause.*)

EDGAR. Would we have any burgundy left in the cellar?

ALICE. No.

EDGAR. But we must have burgundy.

ALICE. What for?

EDGAR. We have to celebrate our silver wedding anniversary.

ALICE. There's no call for us to celebrate our twenty-fifth year of hell.

EDGAR. We sometimes got on well together.

ALICE. You're imagining things.

> (*Longer pause.*)

EDGAR. Soon it'll all be over.

ALICE. Let's hope so.

EDGAR. We're nothing but a barrowload of shit for the rosebeds.

ALICE. Spare me your everlasting barrowloads of shit, will you?

> (*Pause.*)

ALICE. Mail?

EDGAR. Yes.

ALICE. The butcher's bill?

EDGAR. Yes.

ALICE. How much?

> (ALICE *crosses to* EDGAR.)

EDGAR. I need some new glasses.

> (EDGAR *gives* ALICE *the butcher's bill.*)

ALICE. Can you pay it?

EDGAR. Yes.

ALICE. Right away?

EDGAR. Later.

ALICE. If you get sick again you'll be pensioned off, and I'll be the one who has to pay it.

EDGAR. I'm sound as a bell.

ALICE. That's news to me.

EDGAR. A little dizzy spell now and then, that's all.

ALICE. Sometimes, my dear, you are really out of this world. (*She sits down again on the sofa and does her embroidery.*)

EDGAR. I'm good for another twenty years.

ALICE. I doubt it.

EDGAR. I'm not sick. I never was sick. And I never will be sick.

ALICE. That's your story.

EDGAR. I'll die with my boots on, like an old soldier.

ALICE. Not according to the doctor.

EDGAR. The doctor's an imbecile.

> (*Pause.*)

ALICE. The doctor has company tonight.

EDGAR. So what.

ALICE. We are not invited.

EDGAR. Because we won't have anything to do with that lot, and we don't have anything to do with that lot because we don't want to, and we don't want to have anything to do with them because we despise them.

ALICE. Because *you* despise them.

EDGAR. They are scum.

ALICE. You call everybody scum. You are the one exception.

EDGAR. I am a gentleman.

(*Pause.*)

ALICE. A hand of cards?

EDGAR. A hand of cards.

(ALICE *sits at the table. They begin to play cards. Card-playing Scene 1.*)

ALICE. The doctor has the use of the brass band for his party.

EDGAR. Because he crawls to the colonel.

ALICE. You crawl to the colonel yourself.

EDGAR. I don't need to crawl to the colonel, because the colonel thinks very highly of me.

ALICE. But you don't have the use of the brass band.

(*Longer pause.*)

EDGAR. What's trumps?

ALICE. Feeling tired?

EDGAR. No.

ALICE. Then your eyes want seeing to. Spades.

EDGAR. Nonsense.

ALICE. You were saying just now you needed new glasses.

EDGAR. Everybody needs new glasses some time.

ALICE. And you say you're good for another twenty years.

EDGAR. I'm good for another twenty years.

ALICE. Spades are trumps.

(*Longer pause.*)

EDGAR. Six and eight is fifteen.

ALICE. Fourteen.

(*Longer pause.*)

EDGAR. Fourteen.

ALICE. You can't even count now.

EDGAR. When I'm tired, I get absent-minded.

ALICE. But you said you were not tired.

ALICE. To you? Show off to you?

EDGAR. I was a celebrated military man of letters.

ALICE. Who nobody ever heard of.

(*Pause.*)

EDGAR. They're dancing at the doctor's.

ALICE. The Alcazar Valse.

(*Pause.*)

ALICE. The only reason you married was to have someone to show off to.

EDGAR. To you? Show off to you?

ALICE. I was a celebrated actress.

EDGAR. Who nobody ever heard of.

(*Pause.*)

ALICE. I haven't danced for ages.

EDGAR. We're too old for that kind of thing.

ALICE. I'm ten years younger than you.

EDGAR. I'm good for another twenty years.

(*Pause.*)

EDGAR. Bottle's empty.

ALICE. There's no more whisky.

(*Longer pause.*)

EDGAR. It's dark in here.

ALICE. You can't see a thing with those bad eyes.

EDGAR. My eyes are not bad.

ALICE. Then Jenny had better light the lamp.

EDGAR. Jenny won't be coming.

ALICE. Ring.

EDGAR. Jenny's gone.

ALICE. For good?

EDGAR. For good.

ALICE. If Jenny's gone, Christel will be leaving too.

EDGAR. If Christel leaves, we'll never get any more help.

ALICE. It's your fault.

EDGAR. The servants are polite to me.

ALICE. Because you crawl to them, and you crawl to them because you're a despot with the soul of a slave.

EDGAR. I crawl to no one, I have never crawled to anyone, and I never shall crawl to anyone.

ALICE. And you've always got your hand up their skirts.

(EDGAR *sits in armchair.*)

ALICE. Another hand?

EDGAR. No.

(ALICE *sits on the sofa with her back to the audience, starts embroidering again.*)

ALICE. My cousin seems to have made a pile.

EDGAR. The first rich relation in the family.

ALICE. In your family. There are many rich relations in my family.

EDGAR. So that's why your family stinks—they're stinking rich.

(*The teletype machine starts clicking.*)

ALICE. Who's that?

EDGAR. The children. (*He goes to the teletype table. Reads.*)

ALICE. Well?

EDGAR. They're at the main guard post.

ALICE. And?

EDGAR. Judith is sick.

ALICE. As usual.

EDGAR. They need money.

ALICE. As usual.

(EDGAR *sits down behind the teletype table, taps out the closing signal.*)

EDGAR. The children don't work hard enough at school.

ALICE. Since when did you do any work?

EDGAR. I was top of my class. My son flunks every exam and so does my daughter.

20

ALICE. Speak to them.

EDGAR. Speak to them yourself.

ALICE. You're a coward, you've always been a coward, and you always will be a coward.

(*Pause.*)

EDGAR. I *was* a celebrated military man of letters!

ALICE. I *was* a celebrated actress!

(EDGAR *yawns.*)

ALICE. Yawning again.

EDGAR. So what?

ALICE. In front of your own wife?

EDGAR. What else d'you expect? We have this same conversation every evening.

(*Pause.*)

EDGAR. I don't believe your cousin's rich.

ALICE. Yes he is rich.

EDGAR. Then why is he taking the Quarantine post?

ALICE. You never even made it to major.

(*Longer pause.*)

EDGAR. When do we eat?

ALICE. The doctor ordered dinner for his guests from town — the Grand Hotel.

EDGAR. Then they must be having quail. I just wonder what those peasants are drinking with them.

ALICE. Shall I play you something?

EDGAR. As long as it's not your everlasting *Solveig*.

ALICE. Then I won't.

EDGAR. Then why do you ask?

ALICE. The only music you like is your insufferable *Entry of the Boyars*.

(EDGAR *stands and goes to the centre of the acting area.*)

EDGAR. The boyars were gentlemen.

(ALICE *laughs.*)

EDGAR. There are two bottles of champagne in the wine-cellar.

ALICE. I know.

EDGAR. What about bringing them up and acting as if we had company?

ALICE. It's *my* champagne.

EDGAR. Why are you always so stingy?

ALICE. I have to be stingy, because you are not a celebrated military man of letters.

EDGAR. Can't we try to be a little bit nice with one another, just for this evening?

ALICE. Compared with other evenings, we are being nice with one another this evening.

(*Longer pause.*)

EDGAR. Shall I do my dance for you?

ALICE. You're too old for that sort of thing.

EDGAR. If you'll play *The Entry of the Boyars*, I'll do my dance for you.

ALICE. Just because you think everyone else is an imbecile doesn't mean you have to behave like an imbecile yourself.

(EDGAR *sits in armchair.*)

EDGAR. Quail are delicious, as long as they're not cooked in pork fat.

ALICE. The Grand Hotel never cooks them in pork fat.

(*Pause.*)

EDGAR. The colonel thinks very highly of me.

ALICE. That makes him imbecile number one.

EDGAR. Perhaps it would be nice to have company in again.

ALICE. You drive them all away—you give them the creeps.

EDGAR. We used to have quite happy times, when we had company.

ALICE. Not after they'd left. And our visitors felt happy only when it was time to leave.

(KURT *knocks, sitting on the prop bench.*)

EDGAR. That'll be Christel.

ALICE. Go and see.

(EDGAR *goes off upstage right. He comes on again.*)

EDGAR. It's Christel. (*He sits down again in armchair.*) She's leaving too.

(*Longer pause.*)

ALICE. We're done for.

EDGAR. We might as well hang ourselves.

(*Gong.*)

2

ALICE, EDGAR. KURT *enters stage from right.*

ALICE. Round Two.

EDGAR. Company At Last.

(*Gong.* ALICE, EDGAR *and* KURT *greet one another with open arms.*)

ALICE. Welcome, cousin!

EDGAR. Welcome, Kurt!

KURT. Greetings, Alice!

(KURT *embraces* ALICE.)

KURT. Greetings, Edgar.

(KURT *embraces* EDGAR.)

KURT. So you're still living here in this old tower.

EDGAR. Still here.

KURT. With the jail still downstairs.

ALICE. Still downstairs.

KURT. Do you live alone?

ALICE. The children are in town.

KURT. Haven't you any servants?

EDGAR. As free citizens, we don't hold with the enslavement of our fellow creatures.

(*Pause.*)

KURT. We haven't seen one another for a long time.

EDGAR. Fifteen years. We've aged. Grown grey in honourable bondage.

(*Laughter.*)

ALICE. Kurt hasn't changed.

EDGAR. Nonsense. He's aged also. I only hope he too grew grey in honourable bondage.

(*Laughter.*)

ALICE. You're staying here with us.

KURT. I was invited to the doctor's.

EDGAR. That's no place for you.

KURT. The doctor's my superior.

(ALICE *takes* KURT's *coat and hat and hangs them on the clothes rack.*)

EDGAR. Well, old boy, I never let myself be intimidated by a superior.

KURT. I just want to avoid unnecessary unpleasantness.

EDGAR. Stick by me, and you'll have no unpleasantness. On this island, I'm the one who's in command. The doctor's a crackbrained old quack who trembles at the very sight of me. On this island, they all tremble at the sight of me.

ALICE. Almost all.

(KURT *sits at the circular table on Chair 1,* ALICE *on Chair 2.*)

KURT. Right you are, I'm staying here.

ALICE. Till you find a place of your own.

KURT. You make me feel very welcome.

EDGAR. Of course you're welcome. You were bloody irresponsible once. But that's all over now. I'm broad-minded.

KURT. Thank you.

EDGAR. We'll say no more about it. (*He sits in armchair.*)

(*Scene with Visitor.*)

ALICE. You must have knocked about quite a bit.

KURT. I just let myself drift.

EDGAR. And now you've dropped anchor with the pair you had the coupling of twenty-five years ago. Well, my boy, we've kept our marriage going as best we could—oh, now and then we've had words, a real set-to sometimes, it was damned hard going, as it is in any marriage worthy

25

of the name, but Alice here can't complain, the old trouper has rung the curtain down and spends money like water — not for nothing am I world-famous military man of letters.

KURT. I'm glad your textbook on ballistics is still going strong.

EDGAR. It is, and will remain, the standard work, though today the lousy teachers are using a completely worthless new textbook.

KURT. I'm sorry.

EDGAR. It's a scandal.

KURT. It is.

EDGAR. It bodes no good for the future of the Army.

KURT. The main thing is, your marriage is still working.

ALICE. That's so true.

KURT. I'm proud to have had the coupling of you, as you put it old man, though it wasn't quite that.

EDGAR. We'll say no more about it.

(*Pause.*)

KURT. You went abroad.

ALICE. To Copenhagen.

EDGAR. Five times. Did you ever visit Copenhagen?

KURT. I was mostly in America.

EDGAR. I see.

KURT. And in Australia.

EDGAR. It must be frightful in those parts. Inhabited entirely by bandits.

KURT. Well, it's not Copenhagen.

(*Pause.*)

ALICE. What became of your children?

KURT. I have no idea.

EDGAR. Dear Kurt, don't get mad at me. I'm a blunt chap and say what I think. You were wrong to desert your children like that.

KURT. I did not desert them.

EDGAR. It was a shabby thing to do.

KURT. Their mother was given custody.

EDGAR. We'll say no more about it.

KURT. I don't mind speaking about it. I'm glad I weathered the catastrophe.

EDGAR. That's the word. That's the word for it. A divorce is always a catastrophe.

KURT. The divorce? What do you mean? I'm talking about my marriage. *That* was the catastrophe.

EDGAR. What therefore God hath joined together, let not man put asunder. Kurt, we're just worms, poor miserable worms in the face of eternity.

KURT. That's very true.

EDGAR. We have to bear our cross.

KURT. My dear Edgar, you are happily married. You can't possibly understand what an unhappy marriage is like.

EDGAR. My dear Kurt, America and Australia have turned you into a hopeless philistine.

ALICE. Edgar.

EDGAR. A philistine. Anyone who does not bear his cross is a philistine.

KURT. Now listen here—

EDGAR. We'll say no more about it.

(*Longer pause.*)

KURT. How are the children getting on?

ALICE. They attend a school in town and are quite grown up now.

EDGAR. Judith's a fine girl, sound as a bell, and the boy's very bright. He has the makings of a Minister of War.

ALICE. If he gets through his exam.

KURT. Congratulations.

(*Longer pause.*)

27

EDGAR. We hear your children are not very clever.

KURT. Could be. They must take after their mother.

EDGAR. We'll say no more about it.

(*Longer pause.*)

EDGAR. Would you like something to drink?

KURT. Later.

EDGAR. Champagne?

KURT. Tea.

EDGAR. Don't tell me you've become one of those total abstainer hypocrites.

KURT. No, I just moderated my intake a little.

EDGAR. The whole man should go all out.

(*Longer pause.*)

KURT. What about the people on this island?

EDGAR. They are scum.

KURT. Have you made enemies of everyone?

ALICE. Edgar's made enemies of everyone.

KURT. But it must be frightful surrounded by nothing but enemies.

ALICE. That's putting it mildly.

EDGAR. It's not frightful at all. I've nothing but enemies all my life, and they never did me any harm, they helped me. When I kick the bucket, I'll be able to say: 'I owe nothing to anyone.'

ALICE. Life for Edgar was never a bed of roses.

EDGAR. I made myself what I am by my own unaided efforts.

KURT. That's something I can't claim for myself. Ever since I failed to make it as a husband, I lost confidence in myself.

EDGAR. You're a goddamn good-for-nothing.

ALICE. Edgar!

EDGAR. A goddamn good-for-nothing!

(EDGAR *strikes the table.* ALICE *strikes the table.*)

28

EDGAR. Yes, once the machine breaks down, we're nothing but a barrowload of shit for the rosebeds, but as long as the machine keeps rattling on, you should lay about you hip and thigh to find out what makes it tick. That is my philosophy.

KURT. Alice, your husband is simply priceless.

(ALICE *laughs.*)

ALICE. I'm glad you like it here.

(KURT *laughs.*)

EDGAR. You're laughing at me.

KURT. I'm admiring you.

EDGAR. You've come here just to gloat over the unholy mess of our marriage.

KURT. But Edgar, you have a happy marriage.

EDGAR. Even a happy marriage can be an unholy mess. Marriage itself is nothing but a mess. The wind's getting up. (*He goes to barometer table.*) The barometer's falling.

ALICE. You're still staying?

KURT. I'm staying.

ALICE. We eat very simply.

EDGAR. There's a storm blowing up. (*Taps the barometer.*)

ALICE. He's on edge.

EDGAR. I'm hungry.

ALICE. I must go. Talk philosophy till I come back. (*To* KURT) Don't contradict him, or he'll be in a bad mood, and don't ask him why he never made it to major.

EDGAR. Fix something good, dear.

ALICE. Give me money and I'll fix you something good.

EDGAR. Money, money, money!

(ALICE *leaves the acting area and sits on the prop bench left.*)

EDGAR. Money. Money. She's asking for money all day long, until I begin to think I must be made of money. But

when all's said and done, she's a terrific woman, a wonderful woman, and when I think of what your former wife
was like—

KURT. Let's keep her out of it.

EDGAR. She was also a wonderful woman, but you never got
her licked into shape. A man has to get his woman licked
into shape. Licked into shape! (*Sits.*) That's why Alice is
great. In spite of everything.

KURT. Everything?

EDGAR. In spite of everything, because I got her licked into
shape. She's a faithful wife, an incomparable mother, but
she has the very devil of a temperament. My dear, there
were moments in my life when I cursed you for having
coupled me with that woman.

KURT. But Edgar, I did not couple you with her.

EDGAR. We'll say no more about it.

    (*Longer pause.*)

EDGAR. Life is strange. Here I am growing old along with my
wife, staring into the infinite and waiting for the sands of
life to run out. But they are not running out. Because we
have children. Do you too sometimes find yourself
staring into the infinite?

    (KURT *laughs.*)

KURT. No.

EDGAR. Because you don't dare stare into the infinite. Because
you deserted your children.

KURT. I did not desert them!

EDGAR. We'll say no more about it.

KURT. As you wish.

EDGAR. Now you're alone. Alone. Alone. Alone.

KURT. I've got used to that.

EDGAR. Can one get used to being alone?

KURT. Just look at me.

30

EDGAR. You cut a sorry figure.

> (*Longer pause.*)

EDGAR. Forgive me. I like to speak my mind. I can allow myself the luxury of speaking my own mind, can't I? I am the master of this island. Do you know what master means? The Boyars were masters.

KURT. Your good old Boyars.

EDGAR. Masters. They were masters.

KURT. Does Alice still play *The Entry of the Boyars*?

EDGAR. She does.

KURT. Do you still do your dance to it?

EDGAR. I do.

KURT. Nothing seems to have changed much in your lives.

EDGAR. The sands of my life are not trickling away as yours are.

> (*Longer pause.*)

EDGAR. What actually did you do during the last fifteen years?

KURT. All kinds of things.

EDGAR. Did you grow rich?

KURT. Fairly.

EDGAR. I'm not fishing for a loan.

KURT. I'd be glad to help you.

EDGAR. Won't be necessary. Money flows like water in this house. The day when it stops flowing, Alice will leave me.

KURT. You're just imagining things.

EDGAR. That's all she's waiting for.

> (*Longer pause. The teletype clicks.*)

KURT. What's that?

EDGAR. The time signal.

KURT. Don't you have a telephone?

EDGAR. In the kitchen. But whenever we use it, the girl at the exchange tells everyone what we say, so we use the teletype.

KURT. It must be horrible, living on this island.

EDGAR. Life is horrible. (*He laughs, then coughs. He lights a cigar.*)

KURT. Aren't strong cigars bad for you at your age?

EDGAR. I'm sound as a bell. (*Puffs.*) Do *you* smoke? Ah, you haven't the guts for it.

(*Longer pause.*)

EDGAR. Let's talk philosophy.

KURT. I'd rather not.

EDGAR. Let's talk philosophy I said.

KURT. As you wish. (*He sits on Chair 1.*)

(*Philosophical Discussion Scene 1.*)

EDGAR. Do you believe in God?

KURT. In a way.

(*Pause.*)

KURT. What about you?

EDGAR. In a way too.

(*Pause.*)

EDGAR. Do you believe in life after death?

KURT. In a way.

(*Pause.*)

KURT. What about you?

EDGAR. Not at all.

(*Pause.*)

EDGAR. Do you believe that after death there are still wars and rumours of wars?

KURT. In a way.

(*Pause.*)

KURT. What about you?

EDGAR. There's only nothingness. (*He suddenly stares into space.*)

KURT. Yes, in a way—Do you believe— (*He starts.*) Edgar? What's the matter? Edgar!

(KURT *shakes* EDGAR.)

EDGAR. I'll die with my boots on like an old soldier. (*He goes on staring into space.*)

KURT. Alice!

(ALICE *enters left.*)

KURT. Alice!

ALICE. What's up?

KURT. I don't know. Your husband—

ALICE. I know.

(ALICE *kneels in front of* EDGAR, *waves her hand, speaks not unkindly.*)

ALICE. Now then, you old bastard, still staring into that infinite of yours? You've kept me locked up in this tower all my life, I wasted all my life humouring your whims, I wasted my life listening to your twaddle—all my life you've been trying to get the upper hand—but I'm the one who has the upper hand—I'm the one!

KURT. For Christ's sake, Alice, he can hear you.

ALICE. When he's like this he can't hear anything, can't see anything. Go on, kick the bucket, you miserable Boyar, into the rosebeds with you, you barrowload of shit!

(EDGAR *slowly comes to.*)

EDGAR. Did you say something?

ALICE. No.

(EDGAR *gets up.*)

EDGAR. Forgive me. (*He goes to the clothes rack, takes his cap and sabre.*) I have to inspect the guard.

(EDGAR *goes off upstage right and sits on the prop bench at right.* ALICE *sits in armchair.*)

KURT. Is he sick?

ALICE. Very likely.

KURT. Is he losing his mind?

ALICE. Very likely.

KURT. Does he drink too much?

ALICE. He's just showing off.

KURT. There must be something wrong with him.

ALICE. He has these little absences. For months now. And every time he has one, I tell him my mind.

> (*Longer pause.*)

ALICE. Kurt, I invited you to dinner.

KURT. I am getting hungry.

ALICE. We haven't even a dry crust in the larder. We're broke.

KURT. I'll go and buy something.

ALICE. There are no shops open on this island at this time of night.

KURT. A fine sort of island you've landed yourselves on.

> (*Longer pause.*)

ALICE. Kurt.

KURT. Alice.

> (ALICE *rises, brings a photograph album from the piano, sits down near* KURT *on Chair 2. Photograph Album Scene.*)

ALICE. Would you like to see our photograph album?

KURT. Yes, please.

ALICE. I stuck the photos in myself.

KURT. Very nice.

ALICE. Me as Peritta.

KURT. Who's that?

ALICE. A playmate of Medea's.

KURT. Very nice.

ALICE. Me as Eucharis.

KURT. Who's that?

ALICE. One of Sappho's handmaidens.

KURT. Very nice. Your husband as a young second lieutenant.
(EDGAR, *on the prop bench, giving orders.*)

ALICE. If he were to drop dead, I'd bust a gut laughing. As full lieutenant.

KURT. Do you detest one another?

ALICE. Stupendously.

KURT. Since when?

ALICE. Since always. Since I was a virgin bride.
(EDGAR *giving orders.*)

KURT. Very nice. Why actually did you get married?

ALICE. Because he took me. And now I have to polish brass, wipe glasses, scour floors, light fires and cook for him, because the servants are always leaving.
(EDGAR *giving orders.*)

ALICE. Pastor Nielsen. He married us.

KURT. Very nice. You'll seek a separation, of course?

ALICE. We already tried it. Five years we lived in this tower without seeing one another. Then he came whining back to me. The monotony was too much.
(EDGAR *giving orders.*)

ALICE. The colonel.

KURT. Very nice.

ALICE. Our children.

KURT. Very nice.

ALICE. We lost two of them.

KURT. You had to go through all that too?

ALICE. Yes. The other two are still living.

KURT. Very nice.

ALICE. Twins. He eggs on Judith against me, and I egg on Olaf against him. The island, seen from the south.

KURT. Very nice.
(EDGAR *giving orders.*)

KURT. Why does he blame me for your marriage?

35

ALICE. He wants to drive you out of the house. You and your wife with us on the steamer.

KURT. I did not have the coupling of you.

ALICE. It was your wife you married, not me.

KURT. I was in love with my wife.

ALICE. You were in love with me before.

KURT. Yes, but you went off with all flags flying to your military man of letters, to improve your position in society.

ALICE. Stop it.

KURT. We'll say no more about it.

(EDGAR *giving orders.*)

ALICE. My husband as captain. I belong to one damned hell of a sex.

KURT. Very nice.

ALICE. Me with the children on the beach.

KURT. Very nice.

ALICE. If only the ocean would just rise right up and wash us all away. (*Closes the album.*) Kurt, you must stay with me.

KURT. I'll stay with you. I've seen marriage at first hand: my own. Yours is even more disastrous.

(EDGAR *giving orders.*)

KURT. He's finished his inspection.

ALICE. He's furious because there's nothing to eat.

KURT. Take his mind off it. Get him in a good mood. Play something for him.

ALICE. *Solveig's Song.*

(ALICE *sits at the piano, plays and sings.* KURT *leans on the piano, dreamily beating time with his hand. Songs Around the Piano Scene.*)

ALICE. The winter may part, and the springtime fly away, the springtime fly away. The summertime may wither, the year may die away, the year may die away.

(EDGAR *enters.*)

ALICE. You come again to me, yes you're mine, yes you're
mine. I promised to be true. I'll always wait for you,
I'll always wait for you my dear, I'll always wait for
you.

EDGAR. That's enough! (*Slams down lid of piano.*) Is she
complaining again, our Duse who once was praised to
the skies? Did she tell the noble lover of her youth about
her tortured existence in Bluebeard's frightful company?
Get cracking, you old trout, play *The Entry of the Boyars*
before we sit down to table. Your lord has come back to
show you who's master in this house.

(ALICE *takes music from the piano top and places it on the
music rest.*)

ALICE. *The Entry of the Boyars.*

KURT. I'll help you.

(KURT *sits beside* ALICE.)

EDGAR. Come on, get started, I want to dance.

ALICE. *The Entry of the Boyars.*

(ALICE *and* KURT *play four-handed* The Entry of the
Boyars. EDGAR *begins to dance, dances more and more
wildly; suddenly he falls to the ground, and lies there
motionless.* ALICE *and* KURT *continue playing without
noticing what has happened.*)

ALICE. Shall we play it again?

(ALICE *and* KURT *begin* The Entry of the Boyars *again.*
KURT *turns around, sees* EDGAR *lying unconscious on the
floor.* ALICE *turns round.*)

ALICE. Jesus.

(*Gong.*)

3

KURT. Round Three.

ALICE. Dead Faint.

(*Gong.* EDGAR *unconscious in the armchair.* ALICE *in Chair 1 lays out patience.* KURT *sits on sofa.*)

EDGAR. The colonel thinks very highly of me.

KURT. He's talking about the colonel.

ALICE. He's always talking about the colonel.

(*Pause.*)

EDGAR. A grilled mackerel with a slice of lemon.

KURT. He talking about food.

ALICE. He's always talking about food.

EDGAR. Quail.

KURT. Take a deep breath.

(*Pause.*)

EDGAR. What happened?

KURT. You fell down.

EDGAR. I never fall down.

KURT. Nevertheless you fell down.

(EDGAR, *in order to demonstrate his iron constitution, walks round the stage from right to left.* KURT, *anxious, walks backwards in front of him.*)

EDGAR. Was I dancing *The Entry of the Boyars*?

KURT. You were.

EDGAR. How was I—did I dance superbly?

KURT. I was sitting at the piano with Alice and could not watch you dancing.

EDGAR. I always dance superbly. (*He stops.*)

KURT. Take a deep breath.

(EDGAR *breathes deeply.*)

KURT. Are you feeling better now?

(EDGAR *starts walking again.*)

EDGAR. I feel splendid. There's nothing wrong with me. I'm as sound as a bell. (*He stops.*)

KURT. Take a deep breath.

(EDGAR *topples forward,* KURT *catches him.*)

KURT. Alice, come and give me a hand!

ALICE. I cannot bring myself to touch him.

(EDGAR *stands upright again.*)

EDGAR. Something happened?

KURT. You nearly fell over.

(EDGAR *walks on.*)

EDGAR. It's my eyes—they're not up to much now.

KURT. You are sick.

EDGAR. I am not sick, I never have been sick and I never shall be sick. (*He stops.*)

KURT. Take a deep breath.

EDGAR. I feel giddy.

KURT. Take a deep breath.

(EDGAR *walks on.*)

EDGAR. I felt giddy, because the barometer's falling and there's a storm blowing up.

KURT. Lie down.

EDGAR. I will not lie down.

KURT. Then sit down.

EDGAR. I will not sit down.

(*The pair have made a complete circle of the acting area and returned to the place from which they started.* EDGAR *topples over again, is caught by* KURT.)

KURT. Alice! He's your husband and he needs your assistance.

ALICE. Dying requires no assistance.

(EDGAR *stands upright again.*)

EDGAR. What happened?

KURT. Fell over again.

EDGAR. I'm good for another twenty years.

KURT. Take a deep breath!

(EDGAR *sits in armchair.*)

EDGAR. I must sit down. I'll die with my boots on, like an old soldier.

KURT. I'll telephone the doctor.

EDGAR. I'm not having any doctor.

KURT. I'll telephone anyhow.

EDGAR. You can't telephone. They cut the telephone off— the scum.

ALICE. Because we never paid the bill.

KURT. Then I'll go and fetch the doctor.

EDGAR. If he comes here, I'll blast that crackbrained old quack right off the island.

KURT. I'll go, anyhow.

(KURT *leaves upstage right.* ALICE *lays out another game of patience.*)

EDGAR. I'm ill.

ALICE. I've said that all along.

EDGAR. A glass of water.

ALICE. Oh all right.

(ALICE *goes off left, brings a glass of water from the prop bench.* EDGAR *drinks.*)

EDGAR. Much obliged.

ALICE. Now will you take care of yourself?

(*Longer pause.*)

EDGAR. Oh all right.

ALICE. Then take care of yourself.

(*Longer pause.*)

EDGAR. Don't *you* want to take care of me?

ALICE. You can put that right out of your head.

(*Longer pause.*)

40

EDGAR. I'm all washed up.

ALICE. I've said that all along.

(*Longer pause.*)

EDGAR. This is the moment you've always waited for.

ALICE. You've always hoped it would never come.

(*Longer pause.*)

EDGAR. The Boyars were gentlemen. (*He again stares into space.*)

ALICE. Go on, kick the bucket, you miserable Boyar, into the rosebeds with you, you barrowload of shit! You've kept me locked up in this tower all my life, I wasted my life humouring your whims, I wasted my life listening to your twaddle – all my life you've been trying to get the upper hand – but I'm the one who has the upper hand – I'm the one! And another thing – you were never able to shut me off completely from the world as you thought you were doing. I was using the teletype all these years, and you never found out.

(EDGAR *comes to slowly.*)

EDGAR. You said something?

ALICE. No.

EDGAR. I wonder if Kurt's coming back?

ALICE. He wanted so much to accept the doctor's invitation.

EDGAR. He must be at the doctor's now.

(*Pause.*)

EDGAR. I wonder what he's doing now – stuffing himself with roast quail?

ALICE. Kurt won't let *me* down.

EDGAR. Smoked salmon for *hors d'œuvres*?

ALICE. He's not the scoundrel you think he is.

EDGAR. He's a scoundrel and a coward, because he didn't have the guts to say he was fed up with us and that there was grub at the doctor's.

(KURT *enters.*)

41

KURT. The doctor knows all about the state of your health.

ALICE. So what?

(KURT *sits on the sofa.*)

KURT. You must take care of yourself.

ALICE. I've said that all along.

KURT. No cigars.

EDGAR. I'll never smoke again.

ALICE. That'll be the day.

KURT. No whisky.

EDGAR. I'll never touch another drop.

ALICE. That *will* be the day.

EDGAR. What about meals?

KURT. Only milk.

EDGAR. The doctor's a crackbrained old quack.

ALICE. That's what you always say.

KURT. He was very friendly.

EDGAR. The old hypocrite.

KURT. He'll come any time you want him.

EDGAR. Let the bastard get on with his orgies. I'm in the pink. I'm working up a terrific appetite.

KURT. Perhaps he's really feeling better now?

ALICE. He'll soon be off staring into space again.

EDGAR. What's on tonight?

ALICE. Ask Jenny.

EDGAR. Jenny's gone.

ALICE. Ask Christel.

EDGAR. Christel's gone too.

ALICE. Then we won't be eating.

EDGAR. Do you want me to starve to death? (*He again stares into space.*)

ALICE. He's off again.

KURT. I'm really beginning to feel sorry for your husband.

ALICE. What did the doctor really say?

KURT. He's in a bad way.

ALICE. He might die?

KURT. He might die.

ALICE. Thank God for that.

(EDGAR *comes to again.*)

EDGAR. I'm feeling frightful.

ALICE. I've said it all along.

EDGAR. Cognac.

ALICE. We have no cognac.

(*Longer pause.*)

EDGAR. The polonaise.

ALICE. They're really enjoying themselves.

EDGAR. I'm afraid.

KURT. Of what?

EDGAR. Of nothingness.

KURT. Take a deep breath.

EDGAR. I don't want to die.

KURT. Take a deep breath.

EDGAR. I want to live.

KURT. Take a deep breath.

EDGAR. I want to live!

(*Longer pause.*)

EDGAR. Fetch a doctor please, a doctor from the town. Please.

(ALICE *goes to the teletyper. Begins to send message.*)

EDGAR. You know how to do it?

ALICE. I know.

(*Longer pause.*)

EDGAR. Since when?

ALICE. Ages ago.

(ALICE *taps out the closing signal, comes back to the table and starts laying out patience cards again.*)

EDGAR. She knows how to do it. The bitch knows how to do it. (*Falls in a dead faint.*)

43

KURT. Alice.

ALICE. Kurt. (*Goes on with patience.*)

KURT. Your husband—I don't know—

ALICE. Is he dead? (*Goes on with patience.*)

KURT. I think he's in a dead faint.

(*Gong.*)

4

EDGAR. Round Four.

KURT. At the Sickbed.

(*Gong.* EDGAR, *under a rug, lying on the sofa, asleep.* ALICE *in the armchair, powdering her face and doing her lips.* KURT, *behind the circular table, washing his face in a bowl. He has removed his shoes. They are standing in front of Chair 1, over whose back his jacket is draped. His waistcoat is hanging on the clothes rack.*)

KURT. Sun's coming up.

ALICE. He was snoring just now.

KURT. He's recovered consciousness.

(*Longer pause.*)

KURT. He's getting better, God be praised.

ALICE. He's getting better, God damn it.

(KURT *goes to the clothes rack, puts on his waistcoat.*)

ALICE. Is he not singularly repulsive?

KURT. Do you never have a good word for him?

ALICE. Well, he *is* singularly repulsive.

(KURT *goes back to circular table, buttons his cuffs.*)

KURT. He can be quite nice.

ALICE. When he's up to no good.

KURT. He had a hard time of it when he was young.

ALICE. And I'm the one who has to suffer for it.

KURT. Twenty-five degrees below zero and out on the streets without a topcoat.

ALICE. I'd be the same, if I didn't have my old coat from Copenhagen.

KURT. His father squandered every penny he had.

ALICE. As he did mine.

KURT. Yet he loves his daughter.

ALICE. She punched me in the nose.

(KURT *puts his shoes on.*)

KURT. Shouldn't we take his boots off?

ALICE. Take his boots away, there's nothing left.

KURT. Shouldn't I go to the doctor's again —

ALICE. Stay where you are.

KURT. Why do you really hate one another so?

ALICE. Search me.

KURT. But there must be some reason.

ALICE. We're husband and wife.

KURT. He really is singularly repulsive.

(ALICE *has finished her make-up and is gazing thoughtfully at* KURT.)

ALICE. Kurt, I wasn't always very nice to you.

KURT. You were always very nice to me.

(*Pause.*)

ALICE. You're so forbearing.

KURT. Something I learnt from life.

ALICE. Why did you come to this island?

KURT. To take up the post of Head of the Quarantine Department.

ALICE. But you don't need the job.

KURT. Everyone needs some kind of job.

(*Longer pause.*)

ALICE. Why do you want to be the Head of the Quarantine Department?

KURT. To find peace.

ALICE. Are you unhappy?

KURT. Everyone has his problems.

ALICE. Do you still love me?

(EDGAR *wakes up.*)

46

KURT. He's waking up.

ALICE. I'll be in the kitchen. (*She takes the washbowl and goes off left to prop bench.*)

EDGAR. I feel better after that sleep. Was I asleep long?

KURT. You were unconscious a long time, then you fell asleep.

EDGAR. Did a doctor come from the town?

KURT. No.

EDGAR. Scum.

> (KURT *puts on his jacket, takes Stool 1 and sits at the foot of the sofa.*)

KURT. How are you feeling?

EDGAR. The bitch knows how to use it.

KURT. Shall I call your local doctor?

EDGAR. Him? He's sleeping off his hangover.

> (*Longer pause.*)

KURT. Shall I call the chaplain?

EDGAR. What for?

KURT. To ease your conscience.

EDGAR. I have no conscience.

> (*Longer pause.*)

KURT. Shall I call a lawyer?

EDGAR. What for?

KURT. To draw up your will. So that Alice can at least keep the furniture, if something should happen to you.

EDGAR. You mean something could happen to me?

KURT. Something could happen to anybody.

EDGAR. Nothing will happen to me, and if something *did* happen to me, the bitch wouldn't want the furniture.

> (*Pause.*)

EDGAR. I'm thinking.

KURT. What about?

EDGAR. Your wife was a decent sort.

KURT. I suppose.

EDGAR. Unfortunately she had to hit upon a bastard like you.

(KURT *laughs*.)

EDGAR. I believe you were once a bank-clerk?

KURT. Yes.

EDGAR. What did you do in America and Australia?

KURT. I started off as a waiter.

EDGAR. Another messy occupation.

KURT. Then I was in the gold rush.

EDGAR. No job for a gentleman.

KURT. In this life, you sometimes have to go for broke.

EDGAR. It seems you were lucky.

KURT. Fairly.

EDGAR. Now you're going to be the Head of the Quarantine Department, you will of course have your children back to live with you.

KURT. They'll stay with their mother.

EDGAR. One should face up to one's responsibilities.

KURT. Quite.

EDGAR. You are obviously not man enough to do so.

(ALICE *enters with red roses, throws them on* EDGAR's *sofa*.)

ALICE. From the sergeants' mess and the band.

EDGAR. The lower ranks are always thinking of me.

(ALICE *sits in armchair, begins to varnish her nails*.)

EDGAR. Because I'm like a father to them, licking them into shape. They tremble before me and hold me in awe. But, by God, this bluff gesture was well meant. It's got to be well meant.

(*The teletyper clicks*.)

EDGAR. My daughter Judith.

(ALICE *goes to teletyper. Reads tape*.)

ALICE. Tonight grand ball, cannot come, best wishes for rapid recovery. Papa should not drink so much. (*She taps out the closing signal.*)

EDGAR. How miserable this life is! Here I am fighting for life, and my beloved daughter starts taking after her mother.

(ALICE *sits in the armchair again and goes on varnishing her nails.*)

ALICE. You set her against me. Well, now she's turning on you.

EDGAR. Go to hell.

ALICE. There's still justice in heaven.

EDGAR. I can't go on living like this.

ALICE. Then take to your bed.

EDGAR. If I take to my bed, I'll never get up again.

ALICE. You don't *want* to go on living.

EDGAR. I *must* go on living, even if I don't want to go on living.

ALICE. No one's asking you.

EDGAR. I'm a soldier and a gentleman.

ALICE. Then take off those horrible boots.

EDGAR. A soldier should always be ready.

ALICE. Change the record. We're in the throes of peace.

EDGAR. Our marriage is one big bloody mess.

(*Teletyper clicks.*)

EDGAR. The colonel. He thinks very highly of me.

(ALICE *goes to teletyper. Reads.*)

ALICE. Pension granted. (*She gives the closing signal and again sits in armchair.*)

EDGAR. How did the colonel know I was indisposed?

ALICE. Good news travels fast.

EDGAR. I didn't apply for a pension.

ALICE. I applied for it.

EDGAR. I don't follow you.

ALICE. Apparently the colonel doesn't think so very highly of you after all.

EDGAR. The ingratitude!

(*Longer pause.*)

EDGAR. I'm hungry.

ALICE. So what?

EDGAR. Fry a couple of steaks.

ALICE. A couple?

EDGAR. For me and Kurt.

ALICE. There are three of us.

EDGAR. Then fry three.

ALICE. And where am I to get three steaks?

EDGAR. Buy them at the officers' mess.

ALICE. Give me the money.

EDGAR. I have no money.

ALICE. Then we have no steaks.

EDGAR. Get them on credit.

ALICE. We have no credit.

EDGAR. Life is miserable. Miserable. My dear Kurt, for nearly three decades in the service of the fatherland I steeped myself in ballistics and what have I to show for it: I'm starving to death. But perhaps you can't comprehend the misery of existence because you yourself are such a miserable bastard.

ALICE. Edgar!

EDGAR. A miserable, pitiful little bastard.

ALICE. Kurt sat up with you all night on an empty stomach, we don't have any coffee even—and all you can do is insult him!

EDGAR. My dear Kurt, she's furious because I didn't die last night.

ALICE. Because you didn't die twenty-five years ago.

EDGAR, ALICE (*in unison*). Go on, kick the bucket, will you,

you miserable Boyar, into the rosebeds with you, you barrowload of *muck*.

EDGAR. I am not ill, I never was ill, and I never shall be ill.

EDGAR. Damn nice place we have here, damn nice place.

(EDGAR *hands over roses to* KURT.)

EDGAR. And this, old boy, is the marriage you brought about. (*He gets up, goes to clothes rack, takes cap and sabre.*) That's that. I'm going to the mess. Eat steak. Take a stroll in town. Visit the colonel. (*He leaves upstage right.*)

(*Gong.*)

5

ALICE. Round Five.

KURT. A Little Home Music.

(*Gong.* ALICE *playing Chopin on the piano.* KURT *leans on left side of piano.* EDGAR *enters from behind the scenes right.* KURT *waves.* EDGAR *waves back.* EDGAR *hangs his cap and sabre on the clothes rack.* EDGAR *lights a cigar.* EDGAR *goes and leans on right side of piano.* ALICE *finishes the piece.*)

KURT. *Valse de l'adieu.*

EDGAR. Very nice.

ALICE. Well?

EDGAR. What did you two do?

ALICE. We looked round the island.

EDGAR. A measly little island.

KURT. An interesting harbour.

ALICE. And what did you do?

EDGAR. I went into town and had a real blow-out. Nimb's *navarin aux pommes.*

(*Longer pause.*)

EDGAR. You must both be hungry still?

ALICE. We ate at the ferry-landing restaurant.

EDGAR. The food there's frightful.

KURT. Passable.

EDGAR. Ah, well, in America and Australia you can't have found the cooking all that wonderful.

(*Longer pause.*)

ALICE. What's the news in town?

EDGAR. My pension has been granted — retrospectively.

ALICE. Oh.

EDGAR. The colonel thinks very highly of me.

ALICE. How about your health?

EDGAR. I have returned from the Valley of the Shadow.

KURT. And still smoking?

EDGAR. I went to a doctor.

ALICE. Well?

EDGAR. Sound as a bell. I'm good for another twenty years.

ALICE. That'll be nice.

(*Longer pause.*)

EDGAR. The return trip on the steamer was terrific. The sea, the sky, the first stars, the stillness, the peace—the peace of God.

KURT. You've turned pious all of a sudden.

EDGAR. My illness has chastened me.

KURT. Congratulations.

EDGAR. A revelation of the immortality of the soul was vouchsafed unto me.

ALICE. So much for the barrowload of shit for the rosebeds.

(ALICE *again starts to play Chopin.* EDGAR *takes away the music and shuts the piano.*)

EDGAR. My dear Alice, I've finally got our life straightened out.

ALICE. *Our* life?

(EDGAR *goes to the table with the teletyper and puts out his cigar.*)

EDGAR. Our putrid life. (*He sketches a dance step. He goes to sofa.*) Feeling worried?

ALICE. Not in the least.

(EDGAR *laughs.*)

EDGAR. Let's start with my will. You've had it drawn up by a notary, I'll bet. (*He sits on sofa.*)

ALICE. Here you are.

(ALICE *takes will out of drawer in circular table, gives it to* EDGAR.)

EDGAR. Thanks. (*He puts on glasses.*) A new pair of glasses. (*He reads will.*) You stand to benefit.

(EDGAR *carefully tears up will into little strips.* EDGAR *draws* ALICE *to him on the sofa.*)

EDGAR. My dear Alice, on grounds of your oft-expressed desire to put an end to our marriage; on grounds of the lack of affection with which you treat me and the children; and on grounds of the sluttish way you keep house, I have been to town to arrange a separation. So our life is finally being straightened out.

ALICE. Uh-huh.

EDGAR. M-hm.

ALICE. And what is your real motive?

EDGAR. I decided to share the last twenty years of my life with a woman who will love me and bring into my house a little warmth, comfort, attention and beauty.

ALICE. Are you throwing me out?

(EDGAR *laughs and rises.*)

EDGAR. I'm marrying Kurt's former wife.

(KURT *laughs.*)

ALICE. What about me?

EDGAR. I believe you are a celebrated actress.

ALICE. You squandered all my money.

EDGAR. You've a tidy bit salted away.

ALICE. All *you* have is debts.

EDGAR. I have twenty-five thousand crowns in the bank.

(KURT *laughs.*)

ALICE. Here. My wedding ring.

(ALICE *throws the ring at* EDGAR.)

EDGAR. Thanks. (*He puts the ring in his pocket.*) May I request the witnesses to take cognizance of this?

(ALICE *on sofa begins to embroider again, and speaks with a needle in her mouth.*)

ALICE. And may I request the witnesses to take cognizance of the fact that my husband tried to murder me?

KURT. No.

ALICE. Uh-huh.

KURT. How?

ALICE. He shoved me in the water.

KURT. Where?

ALICE. On the bridge.

KURT. When?

ALICE. Two months ago.

KURT. Unbelievable!

(*Pause.*)

EDGAR. You can't prove it.

ALICE. That's what you think.

EDGAR. You have no witnesses.

ALICE. Judith. She'll spill the beans.

EDGAR. She will not. She depends on me, and I on her.

(EDGAR *sits beside* ALICE *on sofa.* KURT *laughs.*)

KURT. You really are an out-and-out bastard. (*He sits at the piano.*)

EDGAR. Your well-brought-up daughter Judith has to have an abortion, because Heaven alone knows who the father is. I am financing the operation, and she will support my version of the accident. After that, she can do as she likes. She is no longer any daughter of mine. I must tell you, she's mortified that you're such an excellent swimmer.

ALICE. She would never listen to me.

EDGAR. We'll say no more about it.

KURT. You have no conscience.

EDGAR. Life has no conscience.

(KURT *plays on piano the first bars of* Solveig's Song.)

EDGAR. Let us pass over in silence your Mama's boy of a son and his boozing and expulsion from school.

ALICE. I was a good mother to him.

EDGAR. Well, let's agree not to talk about the unfortunate by-products of an unfortunate marriage.

KURT. Stop tormenting her.

EDGAR. One should be able to face the truth.

    (KURT *plays on piano the first bars of* Solveig's Song. EDGAR *shakes with laughter.*)

EDGAR. An officer and a gentleman driven to the verge of madness by an actress with no talent—that's the story.

    (ALICE *goes on embroidering.*)

ALICE. I did everything for my children.

    (EDGAR *stands, dignified, sits in the armchair, puts watch on table.*)

EDGAR. Within ten minutes, you will both be out of this house. My watch is on the table.

ALICE. *You* made the children what they are.

EDGAR. Ten minutes. Can you hear fate ticking away? (*He presses his hand to his heart.*)

KURT. What the matter?

EDGAR. Nothing.

KURT. Shall I go to the doctor's again—

EDGAR. I'm feeling bad— (*He falls back in armchair and pretends to be in a fainting-fit.*)

KURT. In a dead faint again.

    (ALICE *embroiders.*)

ALICE. Olaf and Judith would have been better off dead.

KURT. Can I help you?

ALICE. There's no way you can help me.

KURT. Perhaps he's dying.

ALICE. He never dies.

KURT. You mustn't give way now.
> (ALICE *embroiders*.)

ALICE. You don't know the whole story. Fifteen years ago he started an affair with your wife.

KURT. Uh-huh?

ALICE. Are the scales dropping from your eyes at last?

KURT. I knew about it all the time.

ALICE. All the time?

KURT. Well naturally.
> (*Pause*.)

ALICE. He hates you.

KURT. He hates everybody.

ALICE. And you don't want revenge?

KURT. One doesn't need to revenge oneself on a ruin.

ALICE. I want revenge.

KURT. How?

ALICE. He gave himself away. He has twenty-five thousand crowns in the bank.

KURT. He must have pinched and scraped.

ALICE. He blows it all at the mess.

KURT. Then he can't have twenty-five thousand crowns in the bank.

ALICE. I know what to do. He's friends with the quartermaster. The pair of them must have some kind of fiddle going.
> (ALICE *sits on the arm of the armchair and tweaks* EDGAR's *ears*.)

ALICE. I'll send a message to the colonel that you and the quartermaster have misappropriated twenty-five thousand crowns.

KURT. Are you sure?

ALICE. It's the only explanation for such a large sum. You miserable Boyar! (*She goes to the table and uses the teletyper*.)

My husband destroyed my life and ruined my children. He shall sit in the jail underneath this very room and listen to me upstairs dancing *The Entry of the Boyars*. (*She dances.*)

KURT. You're over-excited.

ALICE. Revenge is sweet.

KURT. You're a good dancer.

ALICE. I'm good at other things, too.

KURT. Are you sure?

ALICE. Wait till you get to know me.

KURT. I'd like to get to know you very much.

ALICE. Then you must take your revenge.

KURT. I want to take my revenge.

ALICE. You haven't the guts to do it.

KURT. I have the will to do it.

ALICE. You're much too respectable.

KURT. I'm not at all respectable.

ALICE. Prove it to me.

KURT. Come to bed with me.

(ALICE *stops dancing.*)

KURT. I want to sleep with you.

(ALICE *starts dancing again.*)

ALICE. He could die any moment now.

KURT. Then we'd both be revenged.

(ALICE *and* KURT *leave acting area right, go out of sight.* EDGAR *looks after them, grinning, then dances off left. Gong.*)

6

EDGAR *enters from prop bench left carrying a huge platter of cold cuts and a bottle of wine, puts platter on table, pulls armchair behind table, so that it is now flanked on left by Chair 1, on right by Chair 2. He sits in armchair and tucks a gigantic napkin under his chin.*

EDGAR. Round Six. Dinner Alone.

(*Gong.* EDGAR *says grace, pours out some wine, slowly begins to eat. He drinks, puts glass back on table. Gong.*)

7

ALICE *and* KURT *come from the prop bench right, enter the acting area.*

EDGAR. Round Seven. One Hour Later.

  (*Gong.* EDGAR *continues eating.*)

KURT. You're eating?

EDGAR. Tastes good. (*He continues eating.*) Tastes wonderful.

  (*He continues eating.*)

ALICE. And how long have you been eating?

EDGAR. A long time, and I'm taking my fill. (*He continues eating.*)

KURT. Where did all that meat on the table come from?

EDGAR. From the larder.

KURT. There's not even a dry crust of bread in there.

EDGAR. My dear old boy, I can see you don't know my wife. The food in her larder is piled up to the ceiling.

KURT. Alice, it can't be true.

  (ALICE *lies on sofa, takes a cigarette.*)

EDGAR. While you kept watch all night by my bedside, she kept going to the kitchen to get something to eat. I know her little ways.

ALICE. It's not true.

EDGAR. Strategy. She wanted to play the modest little wife to you. Let's not hold it against her. I've spent many a happy hour in the kitchen while she was asleep. She really seemed to think that an officer and a gentleman never sets foot in a larder.

  (KURT *lights* ALICE's *cigarette.*)

EDGAR. When did you start smoking?

ALICE. Ages ago.

EDGAR. To the colonel. (*He drinks.*)

ALICE. You've made a remarkable recovery.

EDGAR. I'm astonished at myself. Do sit down.

   (ALICE *and* KURT *do not move.*)

EDGAR. A little breast of chicken, my dear?

ALICE. No thanks.

EDGAR. A slice of cold roast beef, old boy?

KURT. No.

EDGAR. What were you two doing all this time?

ALICE. We were inspecting the fortifications.

KURT. Most interesting. (*He leans against the buffet.*)

EDGAR. A masterpiece of defensive architecture. I hope you don't mind my wallowing in this succulent repast?

KURT. Not at all.

EDGAR. To each his own. To the colonel! (*He drinks.*)

ALICE. Did he send a message?

EDGAR. Are you expecting some communication from him?

ALICE. I telegraphed him that you had misappropriated twenty-five thousand crowns.

EDGAR. How did you find out?

ALICE. Easy as pie.

EDGAR. How nice of you to get me thrown into jail.

ALICE. That's your worry.

EDGAR. Our worry.

ALICE. I don't have twenty-five thousand crowns in the bank.

EDGAR. Nor do I. It's the colonel who made himself a present of those. Not that he would embezzle anything: the colonel, to whom his Fatherland owes such a deep debt of gratitude—you can't expect such a man's books to balance all the time, that would be something super-human. I had long been wanting to draw his attention to the deficit: your telegraph message reminded him of it just at the right moment. It must have given him a nasty shock.

ALICE. You lied to me.

EDGAR. Ha! Such a good chap, the colonel. An investigation of my affairs would lead to an investigation of his affairs, and as such an investigation is not politically advisable at the moment, the only course left for him is to grant me a favour.

(*The teleprinter clicks.*)

EDGAR. The teleprinter's started clicking already. You hear that? I've been promoted to major.

KURT. So you finally made it to major.

(EDGAR *folds his napkin.*)

EDGAR. Too late. My dear Kurt, my dear Alice, I am in a precarious state of health.

ALICE. I thought you were sound as a bell again and good for another twenty years.

EDGAR. The doctor I saw in town is of a different opinion. I have only a few months left to live.

ALICE. Ah-ha.

EDGAR. I stand face to face with eternity.

ALICE. And our separation?

EDGAR. What separation?

ALICE. You made arrangements for it when you were in town.

EDGAR. Nonsense.

ALICE. You sounded serious enough about it.

EDGAR. Really? It must have been one of my little jokes. After all, we have to think of the children.

ALICE. Don't bring the children into it.

EDGAR. Why should I bring the children into it? I had a long discussion in town with Judith. She told me of her secret

KURT. Here you are. (*He writes a cheque.*) Fifty thousand dollars.

(KURT *gives* EDGAR *the cheque.*)

EDGAR. Thanks. Now, Alice, you know the kind of man you've saddled yourself with.

(EDGAR *puts the cheque in the breastpocket of his uniform.* ALICE *has counted up her cards.*)

ALICE. Eighty-eight.

(*Longer pause.*)

KURT. That was a rather rotten trick you played on me, old boy.

EDGAR. You wrecked a happy marriage.

KURT. Now look here—

EDGAR. A happy marriage. We were happy together, Alice and I, before you showed up. We lived together, played cards, nattered a bit; she used to play me *Solveig's Song* and I used to dance my *Entry of the Boyars.*

KURT. You tried to murder her.

EDGAR. So what? I frequently felt like murdering her. Every marriage begets murderous impulses. Well. I have to inspect the guard. (*He stands, goes to clothes rack, puts on cap, takes sabre.*) There's only one way to get ahead in this life—liquidate, obliterate, consolidate. (*He sways.*) Then comes the time when one can no longer liquidate, obliterate, consolidate, when there is nothing left but the truth—and the truth is terrible. (*He pulls himself together.*) I can still obliterate! (*He draws his sabre.*) Get the hell out of here, you marriage-wrecker! You are liquidated, you no longer exist for me!

(EDGAR *attacks* ALICE *and* KURT *with the sabre.* KURT *picks up a chair to defend himself with.* EDGAR *staggers, falls on the sofa.* ALICE *calmly begins to build a house of cards on the table.* KURT *sits again.* EDGAR *makes a rattling sound in his throat.*)

EDGAR. Get a doctor.

ALICE. Stop play-acting.

EDGAR. Fetch our local doctor.

ALICE. You're not fooling us again.

EDGAR. Hurry! Hurry!

ALICE. All right, all right.

EDGAR. I'm dying.

ALICE. We've heard that before.

EDGAR. I'm dying.

ALICE. Yes yes yes.

   (EDGAR *rolls over on his back.*)

EDGAR. Please help me.

   (KURT *grins.*)

KURT. Come off it, old boy.

EDGAR. Help. Please.

KURT. Get up. Inspect the guard.

EDGAR. God. Oh God!

KURT. Liquidate, obliterate, consolidate.

EDGAR. I want to live! I want to live!

KURT. You really are a star turn.

   (EDGAR *stops moving.* KURT *goes to* EDGAR, *looks at him, takes the cheque out of his breastpocket and puts it in his own.*)

KURT. Alice, I believe we should have called the doctor.

   (ALICE *is still constructing her house of cards.*)

ALICE. Oh really?

   (*Gong.*)

8

EDGAR *turns the armchair so that its back is towards the audience.*
ALICE *puts a bowl of soup on the table.*

EDGAR. Round Eight.
ALICE. Conversation before Dinner.
> (EDGAR *sits in the armchair with its back to the audience.*
> ALICE *has brought* EDGAR's *greatcoat from the clothes rack*
> *and is sitting on the sofa sewing on his major's insignia.*
> *Gong.* EDGAR *talks incomprehensibly.*)
ALICE. Uh-huh.
> (EDGAR *talks incomprehensibly.*)
ALICE. Mm-mm.
> (EDGAR *talks incomprehensibly.*)
ALICE. Aye-aye.
> (KURT *enters wearing coat and hat.*)
KURT. Greetings, Alice, greetings, Edgar.
ALICE. Welcome cousin.
> (*Longer pause.*)
ALICE. Have you just got back from town?
KURT. I've just got back from town.
> (*Longer pause.*)
KURT. How's Edgar doing?
ALICE. Edgar's doing fine.
> (*Longer pause.*)
KURT. Edgar, I'm glad you're doing fine.
> (EDGAR *talks incomprehensibly.*)
ALICE. He can't talk.
KURT. I see.

ALICE. He's paralysed.

(KURT *gives a cry of surprise*.)

KURT. I'm sorry.

ALICE. He can still hear.

KURT. Very nice. (*He goes to the piano and picks up a piece of embroidery lying on it.*) So you finished your embroidery.

ALICE. Edgar's coat of arms.

KURT. Very nice.

ALICE. I'm giving it to him as a silver wedding anniversary present.

KURT. He'll like that. (*He strikes a couple of chords on the piano, then leans on it at the left side.*) What's that you're doing?

ALICE. I'm sewing his major's insignia on his greatcoat.

KURT. Very nice.

(EDGAR *talks incomprehensibly*.)

KURT. What's he saying?

ALICE. The colonel thinks very highly of him.

KURT. You can understand what he means?

ALICE. I always understand what he means.

KURT. I see.

(*Pause*.)

ALICE. Does he not look singularly impressive?

KURT. A bit pasty.

ALICE. All the same, he does look singularly impressive.

(EDGAR *talks incomprehensibly*.)

KURT. What's he saying now?

ALICE. He's good for another twenty years.

KURT. He bears his cross with fortitude.

ALICE. His mind is still quite clear.

(*Gong*.)

9

ALICE. Round Nine.

KURT. Alice Philosophizes.

(ALICE *sits on the right arm of the armchair.* KURT *sits deep in thought on Chair 1. Philosophical Discussion Scene 2. Gong.*)

ALICE. Life is a puzzle.

KURT. In a way.

ALICE. Edgar once said: It looks as if life is making fools of us.

KURT. Yes, in a way.

ALICE. I have always loved him.

KURT. I suppose you have, in a way.

(*Gong.*)

10

ALICE *sits on the left arm of the armchair (as seen from the audience).* KURT *leans against the buffet.*

KURT. Round Ten.
ALICE. Tending the Sick.
   (*Gong.*)
ALICE. Here, my precious, your nice hot gruel.
   (EDGAR *talks incomprehensibly.*)
KURT. Now what's he talking about?
ALICE. Nimb's *navarin aux pommes.*
KURT. I see.
ALICE. A spoonful for little Judith.
   (ALICE *feeds* EDGAR *gruel.*)
KURT. Alice, I have to leave now.
ALICE. Are you going back to America?
KURT. I'm going back to America.
ALICE. Another spoonful for wee Olaf.
   (ALICE *feeds* EDGAR *gruel.*)
ALICE. Aren't you going to take up your post as Head of the Quarantine Department?
KURT. Someone else is taking it over.
ALICE. And another spoonful for tiny Alice.
   (EDGAR *talks incomprehensibly.*)
KURT. Whatever's he saying now?
ALICE. He says you took back the cheque for fifty thousand dollars.
KURT. So I did.
ALICE. And another spoonful for Pastor Nielsen.
   (ALICE *feeds* EDGAR *gruel.*)

ALICE. Hand it over.

KURT. You want to clean me out?

ALICE. And another spoonful for the quartermaster.

>   (ALICE *feeds* EDGAR *gruel*.)

KURT. I thought you loved me.

ALICE. So what?

KURT. We slept together.

ALICE. So what?

KURT. Well, I just thought —

ALICE. And one more spoonful for the colonel.

>   (ALICE *feeds* EDGAR *gruel*. EDGAR *talks incomprehensibly*.)

KURT. What's he saying?

ALICE. He says people are scum.

KURT. I see.

ALICE. Nice din-din, good din-din, big din-din. (*She puts the bowl back on the table*.)

ALICE. Kurt, hand over that cheque and get the hell out of here.

KURT. And if I don't hand it over?

ALICE. We shall inform the Director of Public Prosecutions.

KURT. You would squeal on me?

ALICE. You're nothing but a petty crook.

>   (*Gong*.)

11

KURT. Round Eleven.

ALICE. Kurt Tells All.

(*Gong.* ALICE *and* KURT *sit on the sofa.*)

KURT. I'm sorry, Alice, I'm not a petty crook, I'm a big businessman. I didn't embezzle a paltry fifty thousand dollars, that was Eriksen. I made millions of dollars. The Director of Public Prosecutions cannot lay a finger on businessmen of my calibre. That's my good Alice. I don't want to bore you with shop talk. Your innocent ears must not hear another word about my business dealings.

(KURT *strokes* ALICE's *hair.*)

KURT. Don't cry.

ALICE. Are you an important person?

KURT. They think very highly of me in certain circles.

ALICE. In what circles?

KURT. In the best circles.

(EDGAR *talks incomprehensibly.*)

ALICE. Shut up!

(EDGAR *is silent.*)

ALICE. What were you doing in town?

KURT. I was talking with the colonel.

ALICE. Will he bag the loot?

KURT. I let him in on a profitable side-job. A quarantine harbour is a very useful sort of place for my merchant fleet.

(EDGAR *talks incomprehensibly.*)

KURT. Now what's he on about?

ALICE. Giving orders.

KURT. I see. The three days I spent with you and Edgar gave me great inner strength. I must confess that I had been rather beset with considerations of a moral nature ... But in this house I recovered my spiritual health. I needed this glimpse into your little world. In the great world in which I operate, life goes on just as it does here: it's only the dimensions that are different.

(*Gong.*)

12

ALICE *stands to the right of the piano,* KURT *to the left.* EDGAR *comes up from behind the armchair.*

EDGAR. Final Round. Farewell Scene.
   (EDGAR *sinks back into armchair. Gong.*)
ALICE. Kurt, take me with you.
KURT. Your place is at Edgar's side.
ALICE. Edgar was once a whole man.
KURT. Yes, of course, on this island he could permit himself that luxury.
ALICE. Kurt, this world is a stinking mess.
KURT. It is men of my calibre who do the least damage in it.
   (EDGAR *talks incomprehensibly.*)
KURT. Now what is he saying?
ALICE. A barrowload of shit for the rosebeds.
KURT. Alice, my yacht's waiting, we must say goodbye. Goodbye for ever. Sing me *Solveig's Song* once more. Then let us part as friends.
   (ALICE *sits at the piano and sings.*)
ALICE. The winter may part, and the springtime fly away, the springtime fly away. The summertime may wither, the year may die away, the year may die away.
KURT. Goodbye, Alice, goodbye, Edgar!
   (KURT *leaves the acting area left.* EDGAR *talks incomprehensibly.* ALICE *sings.*)
ALICE. You come again to me, yes you're mine, yes you're mine. I promised to be true. I'll always wait for you, I'll always wait for you my dear, I'll always wait for you.
   (*Gong.*)